I0756322

FINISHING LINE PRESS
www.finishinglinepress.com

Wishbones

by

Elena Montes

Finishing Line Press
Georgetown, Kentucky

Wishbones

ISBN 979-8-89990-408-0 First Edition

ACKNOWLEDGMENTS

The author gratefully acknowledges Amy Hayutin Contreras for the use of her photographs and likeness as they appear in this volume.

The final poem in this collection, recipient of the Andrea K. Wilson Award for Poetry, was originally published online by Sarah Lawrence College on its Annual Awards and Prizes page (2021) and is reprinted here with permission.

Publisher: Leah Huete de Maines
Editor: Christen Kincaid
Cover Art: Photography by Maria Baranova
Author Photo: Adelin Barstow
Interior Photography: Amy Hayutin Contreras
Cover Design: Elizabeth Maines McCleavy

Order online: www.finishinglinepress.com
also available on amazon.com

Author inquiries and mail orders:
Finishing Line Press
PO Box 1626
Georgetown, Kentucky 40324
USA

Contents

To my mother, stepfather, sister, and grandparents, all of whom appear in this chapbook, thank you for your lifelong support of every project I have undertaken and for the role you all played in shaping the woman I have become today.

Part 1

723 Amsterdam Ave, New York, NY:

People move diagonally through the streets.
They are birds whose lines of flight cross paths—
pursuing warmth, fleeing winter:
a city giving way to barrenness.

I feel the warmth through a windowpane—
Imagine, inside, there is a table set for dinner:
Not a single chair left empty.

In five hours, I will board a plane. I will not sleep because I can never sleep on planes. I will step off the jet bridge and shed layers of clothing.

Once home, I will not be able to flee my heritage—the embarrassment my deficit:
the color of my skin, white like skim milk.

1999—Belén, Costa Rica.

Tropical trees with low-hanging fruits. A beat-up blue bicycle. The house has no door.

Women sit in white plastic chairs, shirts dampened with sweat. Dirt clings to the skin between their toes.

Loud whoops and the noise of tires against dirt.

The men are returning from the fields where they spent the day harvesting sugarcane and melons. Their children greet them, smiling wide and teetering as they run up to grab at the men's legs.

One child is tossed lovingly into the air, hanging naked and weightless, before being caught in the bassinet of her father's arms.

~

I was born 3 months before the February heatwave of 2002 broke temperature records in Los Angeles. Our little yellow house lacked air conditioning, so my father poured cool water over my head in the kitchen sink. I cried and cried, already accustomed to the tepid weather my birthplace was known for, relying on others to settle my tiny pink body.

There was the mantra of my persistent wail, the rhythmic hum of the pump pulling milk from my mother's breast,

My grandmother laughing in the other room, and the lullaby of my father's voice as he sang my song to me:

Mi niñita bonita, mi Elena Sofia.

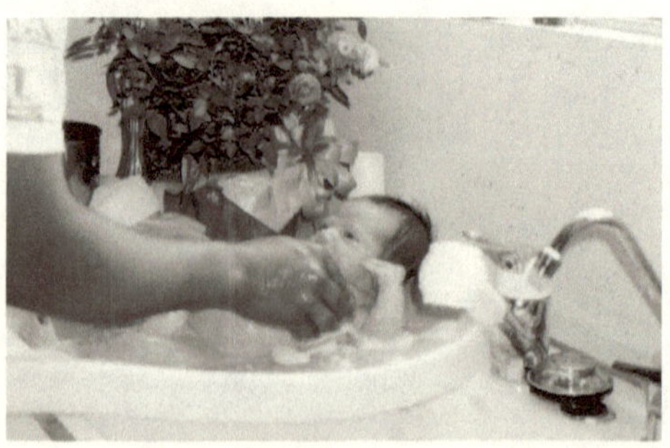

Santa Monica, the beachside city where my grandparents bought their first house. Where my mother grew up and where she gave birth to me:

I am two years old. I have been lying awake in my crib for an hour, staring at a small glowing night light shaped like a moon. The front door opens and then closes again. My mom is talking, in hushed tones, to someone who is not me. It is a man.

I let out a few small sniffles. There is laughter.

"She won't go to sleep," my mother says.

When she doesn't come to get me, I bring the small stuffed bunny my father gave me to the locked gate, stuff her through the railing, and watch as she tumbles down the carpeted staircase.

"Mom," I call. "Mom, Help. Kiwi fell."
Silence.

I shake the gate until I hear a chair scoot and see my mother carrying Kiwi back up the stairs.

"It's time to go to bed," she says, taking me by the hand and leading me back to the dark room.
"Who is here," I ask.
"A friend," she replies, tucking me in and leaving me again, even though she knows I am still awake.

Another bedtime Story: "'*Despierta, despierta, levántate,*' your father yells. A scorpion had crawled from the open window into the bed and stung him in his sleep. I flung the covers from the cot, sending the black creature soaring."

'What did it look like?" I ask.

"Black and big and shiny," my mother replies, lifting her hands above her head and baring her teeth.

I prop myself up on my knees, "Then what? Then what happened?"

My mother draws out her words, "then…." She leans in and kisses me on the forehead, tucking me into bed. "Your father called the doctor, and he said the big ones aren't poisonous. I wasn't allergic, so we were all going to be okay." She turns off the light.

"Wait! Mommy, tell it again."

Other things I remember: Falling on the pier dock, scraping my knee. The difference between double and triple A batteries, an angry sky.

Origami paper planes, flower soap that melts underneath the faucet, and the first necklace I ever owned: a choker with a hand-carved quartz bear my father made me. The identical necklace he gave me when I grew too big to wear the first.

Photographs pulled from a dusty shoebox: a worn-out shirt, a summer's day in the banana fields. His blurred figure riding a bull.

Feelings: callused hands rubbing my back, the warmth of my parent's bodies pressed against me as I fell asleep, and then the warmth of only one body, my mother's.

Drawing pictures of the three of us holding hands, crying when my mom couldn't make pupusas the way my father did.

Her telling me, "Daddy drinks too much. He is sick. You can't see him until he gets better."

Asking for more stories, keeping pieces:

"Your father is a fisherman. Once, he caught a baby hammerhead shark with nothing but a plastic bottle and a piece of twine."

"Boy, can he dance. You get that from him."
And "He always makes everyone laugh. He made you laugh."

I wrote letters that my mother never sent:

I miss you, Papito. Please stop drinking so I can see you.

Te amo,
Elena

~

I know my father's story in the way you know historical facts. The timeline. The main events.

I watch how he moves in home videos: the choreography of him pouring his coffee, biting a small piece of plantain, and feeding it to me on a pink plastic spoon.

His love, his touch, his language, my language is a foreign tongue. After he left, I felt him next to me.

Then, I felt no one at all.

It's 1988. My father has been working in the fields since he was in the fifth grade, when he dropped out of school and moved from his hometown in Belén to Batán. There, he lived with a distant aunt and sent his weekly earnings home to his mother, brothers, and sisters.

The worst jobs were in the fields, where my father spent most of his childhood. By 18, his girlfriend, Elisa, was pregnant with their first child, my half-brother Antonio.

Then, my father began working both jobs. He would harvest during the day and pack the produce at night. They had two more children, boys named Arlando and Luis.

At some point, my father and Elisa broke up. I don't know this part of the story.

My mother moved to Batán to open a school while volunteering for the Peace Corps. It is here that my parents will meet.

Part 2

A note on translation: You can't write about the loss of language using the language you've lost. I script my life often. The me on one page is never quite the same as the me on another. I am afraid of what I don't remember.

I mean, I am afraid to hear it, to see it, and to speak it wrong.

Names: I was El-en-a, Elenita. We used Spanish vowels when I was a baby—for a couple of months. Ahava Ghilat, meaning joy, was the name given to me by a Rabbi. I belonged to a temple and was baptized in a church.

In preschool, I was called A-lain-a because it was easier for my white teacher to say. Last name Montes, meaning mountains. Like the Cordillera Volcánica, which overlooks the town where my father was born.

Santa Monica 2000. It is my father's first Shabbat. He is terrified of his wife's family, and the china, and the tradition he doesn't recognize.

"Grandma insisted Papito pour the wine," my mother recounts. "It was a sort of peace offering to me from her. But his grip on the bottle slipped, and wine spilled all over grandma's fancy tablecloth."

I gasp. My mother is not telling this like a silly story.

"We all said it was fine. And you know Grandpa, he started to laugh. Grandma and I sprung up and tried to sop up the rest of the mess. And then we were all laughing because what are the odds that the wine spills in the middle of a prayer."

I am smiling now too, imagining the scene playing out.

"But your father, he started to cry. He was so embarrassed. I didn't know what to say. I didn't know how to console him."

~

The last time I saw my brothers was before,
before my absence of language and my father's first absence
from my life:

We all drove to the airport in my mom's blue pickup truck. My brothers arrived straight out of customs, where they presented B-2 tourist visas. We took them to our little house, my first house, with a rickety hand-made fence and walls speckled like a robin's egg.

We visited all the textbook places: Disneyland, Universal Studios, and the Hollywood Walk of Fame. I learned later that this was supposed to be their introduction to Los Angeles, to their new life, in a new city, with a new sister.

I do not remember the trip—only the feeling:

The room, I lived in for 8 days with all my brothers.
How they would come in the morning and lay their hands on my back as I woke.

"Despierta Elenita, despierta," they'd whisper.

3 years later, my father has just gotten out of rehab. I visited him in a halfway house with a communal backyard.

A Definition: Mi Media Naranja, meaning my other half.

My father plucks an orange from the tree—
Human beings used to be orange-shaped, he says.

From his back pocket, he pulls a knife,
And separates the globe into two perfect halves.
Eso es mio y esto es para ti.

Mira…las caras.

The juice from my half went into one cup.
His juice went into another.
One teaspoon of sugar

Two cubes of ice

El azucar se hace con sangre.
Sugar is made from blood.

~

2005. My father lives in a great big house that smells like tortillas. It has a porch, and a front yard, and the woman next door grows soursop and makes me agua de guanábana.

It is Sunday, and I am sitting on the brown couch watching Toy Story. My thighs stick to the hot leather. The boli I am eating is running down my hand and making my arm sticky. I lick the melted ice cream. Coconut is wedged between my teeth.

Rex sees a light, and he thinks it's the way out. Woody says no, it's not daylight; it's the incinerator. The toys are about to fall into an enormous fire.

I know what's going to happen, but I am still scared.

My father goes to the kitchen and opens a beer. I never tell my mother.

Other details: the night my father snuck me into the local dance bar and taught me how to salsa. Making lemonade only we could drink because we both preferred it with salt instead of sugar.

Eating pan con dulce hot, straight out of the oven and dipping it in coffee so sweet, it would make your nose crinkle.

My father swinging the door open to his office and asking me what color I wanted to paint it.

"Pink," I yelled. "Pink!"

The little white dresser with hand-painted roses—the first time I got a drawer to keep my clothes in at his house.

And then, the day I came home from school, my mom waiting for me by the front door.

Thinking, she had a surprise planned for me, when she asked if I wanted ice cream before dinner. Knowing, the news was bad when she started to cry.

Imagining My Father Dead:

I. The first time I wondered if you were dead, I was sifting through boxes of old books, and came upon one you used to read to me: *Ladder to the Moon.*

Is it lonelier to grieve or lonelier to be angry?

I put the book in the donation pile, and the moon
you gave to me so many years ago,
grew smaller inside of me.

It shrank into nothingness,
And I was never again whole.

II. The second time I wondered if you were dead, I was standing on the red dirt floor of your childhood home. Your mother asked me how you were.

People, faces I didn't recognize, spoke at me.

My native tongue fell into my open hands.
I wanted to say something, but they couldn't understand.

I was a stone, falling, falling into a well,
in which no one could hear me.

~

The First School, Portrait Day:

Here I am, posing,
Hair escaping its elastic.
Peach fuzz sprouts from my head in a halo.

Yellow and green toy car with a gimp wheel,
painted pathway, great big oak tree.
One hand is clamped in a fist behind the little white body
in a dress shirt.

I will not lose my front teeth until I am 8.
Then, my tongue will poke through the cavity in my mouth
when I try to pronounce my t's
Tiempo, tierra, tradición—

There will be a new house, with a new bed, and a new man to
shelter me from your leaving.

Part 3

I am 4, sitting on my grandmother's lap during the ceremony, pinching the loose skin on her elbow. It is squishy and warm, and I don't understand why everyone is crying. My stomach is making a funny gurgling noise, and I wish my grandmother would let me eat the goldfish she has stowed away in her purse.

My mother and the man I also call my father say a bunch of words, and then he stomps on a crumpled-up towel. It makes a loud, crunching sound.

He is calling my name and reaching his hand out. I don't want to go in front of everyone, but Grandma pushes me off her lap, and then I am standing there, and everyone is staring at me, and I have no other choice.

I bury my face in my mother's gown. The fabric is itchy, and it smells funny—like bleach.

My stepfather begins, "*Not only is Amy a remarkable woman, she is also a remarkable mother. Her body and her guidance have produced a most extraordinary little girl, who, from this day forward, I will have the great, great pleasure of introducing as my daughter. It is the role of a father to offer support and guidance so that his children may have the opportunity to grow and thrive and prosper. It is the obligation of a father to continually strive to be an example of what he wishes his children to be: kind and thoughtful, charitable and honorable, fair and honest. And it is the duty of a father to love his children without condition or constraint.*"

I am 5. My stepfather is wheeling my mother into the living room in a strange black chair. She is resting her head on her hand, looking at her lap. But there is nothing there—just a dark blue blanket.

They look sad. My grandparents, who were watching me while they were gone, look sad, too.

"We lost the baby," my mom says.

How does someone lose a baby, I wonder. *Did he fall out of her? Had he crawled out of her belly button while she wasn't looking? Would they lose me?*

I was too afraid to ask for the answer.

Then, I am 6, waiting in a dimly-lit hospital lobby with a TV. My grandfather waits with me. The chairs are big and green and itchy. At some point, I fall asleep, and then strong arms carry me into another room.

I wake up, and my sister is there, small and loud.
My parents tell me her name is Melanie.
I want to squeeze her, to bury my face in her face, and kiss her tiny little brown eyes while she sleeps.

Gentle, my mother says. *Gentle.*

~

Luis went away suddenly. Antonio, Arlando, and my father went away too. But they went away the way most things go away—slowly. I never knew any of them. At least, I cannot remember knowing them. I cannot remember loving them. Mostly, I remember needing them, which must be an extension of love.

2006, the day my mother gave me ice cream before dinner:

> A stray bullet barrelled through the air—
> Gliding through the adolescent body of a boy.
> Leaving behind a uniform channel through which he would vanish
>
> Alone, in an alleyway, no one would remember the name of.
> His father, my father, would not recognize the wound
> As if it is was too narrow for my brother's life to have escaped through.

2007. I am alone on the front porch, expecting my father to swing open the door, late like he always does, still in his boxers. The sun is touching the mountains. Soon it will be dark.

Then, rain, thunder. The chalk I left out on the sidewalk the weekend before is swimming in a small puddle.

Lightening, like the flash of a camera, illuminates my father's vacant bedroom.

Other memories: My sister pushing off the ground to stand on her own two legs, wobbly as an uneven table, the bark of a neighbor's dog, the taste and smell of chlorine, sharp like bleach.

The big play structure my step-father built: the green slide, the black swing with metal chains that get hot in the sun.

Getting my first splinter, learning that the tooth fairy isn't real, making my best friend cry. Then telling her, "Don't be such a baby."

Vomiting on my favorite pair of blue duck socks, the song my step-father sang me when he put me to sleep.

~

The next time I see my father I am 7. When we finally reach the San Diego Zoo, the thermostat in his little grey Sedan reads 104 degrees.

I bee-line for one of the little ice cream carts when we finally make it inside. I am still smacking on the bubble gum you get to eat once you've finished the cone, when my father grabs my hand and leads me to where they keep the bulls.

I climb up onto the bottom rung of the railing. The metal is hot, and the fresh paint sticks to my forearms.

"One day, I'll take you to our home," my father says, "We will take a bus to Zapote." He waves his hands over the railing.

“Imagine thousands of horses and men in sombreros con diamantes brillantes; big carnival rides. Everyone’s laughing and dancing and singing…and then, right in the middle of it all, the bulls.”

I try to brush the paint off my forearms, but it’s just mixing with my sweat and getting stuck in my arm hair. My father uses his hand to tilt my chin in the direction of the enclosure. He points to the big brown animal rolling in the dirt. It looks funny, like a cow missing its spots.

Then, yelling. My father is crying, and I don’t know why, and that is making me cry.

My face is hot, and my hair is wet with sweat. I’m saying I’m sorry, and I don’t know what I’m saying sorry for.

He’s yelling louder, and I’m only catching every few sentences because he’s saying every other word in Spanish, and I don’t speak Spanish anymore.

I tell him I can’t understand him, and that makes him even angrier. He says he spent a lot of money on the tickets. He says I didn’t even have any fun.

I’m trying to make him feel better. “I did. I did,” I say. I’m crying harder now. “Dad, it’s just really hot. That’s all I’m just hot.”

~

Christmas: I let myself into my father’s house through the garage. It is dark, and it smells of sweat, dirt, and old beer, lingering like burnt rubber.

I clock the tree we put up the weekend before sitting in the corner of the room. I want to go home—to the mercury glass ornaments my grandmother passed down to us and the incandescent bulbs that lit our tree—the tree I knew.

I approach the wall, brittle needles crunching beneath the soles of my feet, and shove the bent prongs of the plug into the wall socket.

The lights are oppressive, white, blinding, illuminating a dead tree and a basin drained of water. I call for my father.

No answer.

Just the clanking of the heater and the sound of my own breathing.

Part 4

D Train, Broadway, Lafayette: A man on the subway jams a wad of chewing tobacco between his cheek and molar, stirring my memory: the smell of sweetened breath. The sound of spit hitting the pavement next to my shoe.

It's 2015. My best friend's room is small and purple. Inside is a bunk bed she shares with her younger sister and a mirrored closet door that remains perpetually ajar. The shelves overflow with clothes: winter clothes and summer clothes and too-small clothes and silver sequined purses and stuffed animals she tried to rescue from the mouth of her black lab, Penny.

Our mothers have decided it is *okay* to leave us home alone.

"That is your room," May says, sliding the closet door open and using her arm to sweep the top shelf clear.
"Okay then, I'll be the girl, and you be the boy," I say.
"No, I want to be the girl," she replies
"Fine then. I'm the boy, and that's your room, and I'm knocking on your window."

May clambers up the shelving unit, ducking under the door frame and curling into a ball on the top shelf. I shove the door closed, squishing a stuffed monkey that had fallen to the floor, and knock.

She opens up.
"Shh, you have to be quiet so my daddy doesn't hear, or he'll come and get you."
"Let me in," I whisper.

I lean my back against the cold metal surface of the door frame. My feet are on the bottom shelf. My face is a few inches from May's. We give each other a wet slobbery kiss. Her lips are soft and pillowy and warm. I feel like I've done something terrible.

"Now what," I whisper.
We kiss again.

Then it's a Sunday:

My father takes me to church—his shame projects onto me.

An invisible sheet through which I will see myself, and the world, and the women I will one day love.

I regurgitate prayers in a language I no longer understand
and get embarrassed when I dip my hand
          too far into the holy water—
map the cross out on my chest backward.

Gringa, gringita, tu piel es tan hermosa,
I am once again with   out.

But when he thinks I get the prayer right, my father smiles
and winks at me. I am concealed by my ability to open and
close my mouth, wordlessly—
Like a baby learning.

~

Other memories: our first family trip to Mexico, the street vendor who braided red ribbons into the ringleted strands of my sister's hair, her skin, toasted.

"Brown brown berry," my mother and step-father sang.

Realizing, you could be Hispanic even if you didn't speak Spanish. Realizing, that Hispanic people who can't speak Spanish make other Hispanic people sad.

The first time, I was allowed to walk around the mall alone with my friends. A strange old man looking at me for a little too long in all the wrong ways.

The bumps on my face. The bumps on the back of my mother's arms. The pink birthmark between my sister's eyebrows. Shaving with a rusty razor. Cutting my leg. Getting scared and confessing to my mother.

I am 14. I look at the clock. It's 3:00 am. My father is shaking me awake. He has my purple suitcase already packed in his hand.

"We are leaving now," he tells me.

I'm confused because we are on a trip to Arizona with his girlfriend and are all supposed to fly back together tomorrow.

He says it again, "Get up. We are leaving now."
"Where's Maria," I ask.
"She's asleep. Come on, hurry up."
"Is she coming?" I repeat.
"No," he says, and he's still whispering, but I can tell he's angry.
I know that means I'm supposed to stop talking now.

I get into the Uber, still in my pajamas. My dad tells me our flight isn't for another couple of hours, so after we make it through security, we sit at a cafe with a big neon sign that reads "Sip, Coffee, Beer."

I get an orange juice. My dad gets a Corona. Then another, and another. He is talking to me again.

Then he is crying and saying he misses my mother, and I'm embarrassed because we are in the middle of the airport, and everyone is looking at us. I want him to stop talking, but he doesn't.

At some point, I fall asleep.

Later: "What time is it," I ask my dad. The gate where our flight was supposed to leave is closed. There's nothing on the board.

"6:00 am," he replies.
"Fuck," I whisper, getting up and wandering over the concierge. I know she is going to tell me the last call for our flight was 30 minutes ago.

I call my mom to let her know our bags would be arriving before us.

She is annoyed because I booked the new tickets using her credit card.
"You have to listen for the boarding call, she says."

"I know. Sorry," I reply, leaving out the part about my father being drunk.

~

I'm 15. It's night. We are in Malibu. My boyfriend is speeding up the canyon because I was supposed to be home an hour ago.

I stick my hand out the window, waving it in the breeze. My face is hot, and strands of my hair are sticking to my lip gloss.

I tell him to drive faster. The lights are blurring. He runs over the edge of a curb and swallows his chewing gum.

"That's going to take 8 years to digest," I laugh.

He's two years older than me, and I am drunk on wine. I know he wants me, and that makes me feel beautiful.

Adolescence: Kissing a man who tasted like cigarettes, tasting myself when I kissed a girl who smelled like vanilla.

Hairspray in my mouth. Lipstick on my teeth

Pooling cash tips from working weekend shifts at the salad shop to buy a fake ID, slapping it down onto the glass checkout counter of the local liquor store.

Beer spilling on my white shirt, beer spilling down the back of my dress, calling my friend crying after I scratched my mother's car.

Calls going unanswered and unreturned. Relief when my father said he didn't want to see me anymore.

Writing letters again. Refusing to send them:

Sometimes I think the worst of me is the worst of you. I place your picture face down when my friends come to visit. And I know, I know the things I take for granted someone else is praying for.

I straighten and then curl my hair, which rests like a noose on my collarbone.

I make dinner. I say grace by myself

I wait for you.
I wait
I wait.

Notes on Desire:

Desire as indignity is desire as steam
rising from the still-wet body.

A boy in striped swim shorts lying by my poolside.
The desire to watch—To be watched.

There was desire for a stranger—
Desire for the palm of a hand pressed firmly against the inner thigh,
The desire to touch and to be touched.

Desire at daybreak, awaking in the oppressive linen
of someone else's bed—
Desire to flee and desire to be forgotten.

Desire at dusk—in slender fingers packing a log of tobacco into paper
Desire as anticipation—
Guilt and a desire for more desire.

Part 5

2020. Leaving LA—If I didn't care, I wouldn't be writing.
When will I be home again? I don't know:

> Grey shirt, grey sweatpants, the grey of the wool blanket I'm wrapped in—the grey of the shadow cast over this page.
>
> Grey eyeliner borders my brown eyes, brown like my father's and brother's, the Lohman brown chicken and her brown eggs. Then the ringing brown wall phone, its subsequent silence; black, and then red. Black as the bottom of a waterless well.
>
> Red as desperation and red as anger. Red in writing: red as a rose, red as a pomegranate, red as the cardinal that marks the beginning. Red red paranoia that slinks like a corn snake appearing beneath my pillow when I least expect it. Red as my wound.
>
> White coats open, they sort through the bad parts and stitch me back up again. The world is white. White like light, white like heaven, white as the popcorn walls in my first apartment.
>
> White as the hand-me-down wedding dress I steal from the back of my mother's closet. Something new, something blue. Baby blue like the suit. Like the pen I use to define a self, I am outside of.

9:45pm, Cheap Hotel Room, in which I Decide to Write about god:

> My last summer as a child is ending.
> Outside, the air is still except for mosquitos buzzing.
> They stick to the glue mat affixed to my window.
> I want to stop seeing—
>
> The living climbing over the dead.
> *Marigolds, a forgotten jacket, rainwater, you.*

Feelings: Hot coffee burning my tongue, my first snowfall, a big glass of ice water in the summertime.

Bésame Mucho and carnitas in the backyard. My father, grinning. The time I bit into a jalapeno and told him my mouth felt like it was buzzing.

~

I'm a young woman walking around Central Park past my bedtime. The lights are on at the ice rink. A couple is speaking Spanish.

I know more about the homeless man on the bench I pass daily than my father. I know what he eats and when he drinks. I know when to be worried if he doesn't come home:

Wishbones

Tell me about the dream,
    Where we dig the bodies from the dirt.

We dig the bodies from the dirt,
    And bring them back home.

What is home,
    If not, a place you try to give back to yourself?

I try to give myself some hope
    And run my finger along the wishbone

My brother and I broke two sides of the wishbone.
    He told me to keep a piece for good luck.

After Jericho Brown

With Thanks

This chapbook is the product of ongoing conversations with my writing advisors and family. Together, we reflected on the struggles of our younger selves and the role of narrative in shaping personal identity. It would not exist without the contributions, compassion, and honesty of a village of supportive individuals whose guidance and dedication helped bring this project to life.

Jeffrey McDaniel—a gifted poet and my advisor throughout college—has been a mentor since the beginning of my journey at Sarah Lawrence College. He was the first person I met upon arriving in New York, and his support has extended far beyond the classroom. Thank you for your insightful line edits, your constant encouragement to share my work, and your presence during a difficult period in my life.

Stephen O'Connor, a writer whose fiction, nonfiction, and poetry I greatly admire, introduced me to the power of simplicity in storytelling. His Fact or Fiction class first sparked my interest in hybrid forms. Without the countless hours he spent outside the classroom providing advice, feedback, and a listening ear, I would not have been able to produce the work you are reading today.

Scott Shushan, a published professor of aesthetics and moral psychology, helped me probe the deeper purpose behind this chapbook. His guidance throughout my philosophy studies, especially on the subject of narrativity, transformed from a collection of disparate poems into a cohesive work.

Elena Montes is a Costa Rican–American poet, fiction writer, and visual artist whose work explores the emotional and psychological landscapes that shape identity. She grew up splitting time between her parents' homes in a predominantly Hispanic neighborhood in Inglewood and on the Westside of Los Angeles, an experience that continues to inform her writing about culture, memory, and belonging.

After moving to New York, she attended Sarah Lawrence College, where she earned a Bachelor of Arts in the liberal arts with concentrations in creative writing, philosophy, and race theory. In 2024, she received the Andrea Klein Wilson Award for Poetry for two poems that appear in her debut collection, *Wishbones*.

Montes works in a hybrid form that blends poetry, prose, and image, pushing against traditional genre boundaries. Her writing inhabits the in-between—between languages, between image and text, between inheritance and self-definition—interrogating how memory is shaped, fractured, and reclaimed.

www.ingramcontent.com/pod-product-compliance
Lightning Source LLC
LaVergne TN
LVHW090541110826
845146LV00003B/1222

* 9 7 9 8 8 9 9 9 0 4 0 8 0 *